W9-BJP-622

Knox County Public Library
502 N. 7th St.
Vincennes, IN 47591

Cornerstones of Freedom

First Ladies

Susan Maloney Clinton

CHILDRENS PRESS®
CHICAGO

Library of Congress Cataloging-in-Publication Data

Clinton, Susan.
The first ladies / by Susan Maloney Clinton.
p. cm. – (Cornerstones of freedom)
ISBN 0-516-06673-0
1. Presidents' spouses– United States–Juvenile literature. [1. First ladies.] I. Title.
F176.2.C57 1994
973'.099–dc20 93-36995
[B] CIP
AC

Printed in the United States of America.

2 3 4 5 6 7 8 9 10 R 03 02 01 00 99 98 97 96

The First Lady—the wife of the president of the United States—has one of the most interesting positions in American public life. The First Lady is not elected, yet she can have great influence and power. She is the ultimate insider, yet she must be very careful about saying what she thinks. No laws dictate what a First Lady must do, yet the list of things she should do is always growing. She should be able to entertain both visiting heads of state and visiting troops of Girl Scouts; the president's backers and his opponents. People expect her to understand the problems of farmers, inner-city children, small-town mayors, and international corporations.

First Lady Mamie Eisenhower holds her first press conference, in March 1953.

Angelica Van Buren and Harriet Lane

Martha Jefferson served as White House hostess for her widowed father, President Thomas Jefferson (1801-09).

Meanwhile, her private life becomes public property; her home is home to the nation.

The job is complex and demanding, but no experience is required to become First Lady. Young women have filled the role; so have mature women, well-educated women, and women of very limited education. Not all the First Ladies have been presidents' wives. For example, bachelor president James Buchanan had his niece Harriet Lane fill the role. Widower Martin Van Buren relied on his daughter-in-law Angelica to be his hostess.

Some First Ladies have been wealthy; others worked hard to make ends meet. Julia Grant went from struggling on a barren farm called

Note to the reader: Each time a First Lady is introduced in this book, the inner margin will show you the name and term of office of the president who was her partner.

James Buchanan (1857-61)

Martin Van Buren (1837-41)

Ulysses S. Grant (1869-77)

"Hardscrabble" to hanging crystal chandeliers and hosting twenty-nine-course dinners in the White House.

A First Lady cannot win the job in her own right, but she can succeed at it in her own right. Public opinion is a good measure of a First Lady's success. A well-liked First Lady can win support for her husband. Her influence with voters and lawmakers can help the president get things done. Some First Ladies have been more popular than their presidential husbands. Others have drawn public dislike and distrust.

A First Lady's popularity depends not so much on what she does as on how she does it. The public responds to the First Lady's style.

Julia Grant (seated in center) with husband Ulysses (seated at left) and other members of the Grant family in 1870

Jacqueline Kennedy (above) and Elizabeth Monroe (right) brought elegance to the White House.

However, times and styles change quickly. That is why there is no recipe for a successful First Lady. The American public has liked lighthearted and extravagant First Ladies as well as serious and frugal ones. The cool, elegant Elizabeth Monroe irritated the public of her day, while the American people admired the same traits in Jacqueline Kennedy.

James Monroe (1817-25)

John F. Kennedy (1961-63)

Different approaches have worked for different First Ladies. During World War I, Edith Wilson wanted to share in the sacrifices Americans were making. So the White House had meatless days just like any other American household. Mrs. Wilson also saved money for the war effort by

Woodrow Wilson (1913-21)

Edith Wilson

Sheep on the White House lawn during the Wilson administration

John Tyler (1841-45)

letting a herd of sheep crop the White House lawn. Young, beautiful Julia Tyler took the opposite approach. During her receptions, she sat on a raised platform with a diadem in her hair, surrounded by a dozen maids of honor in matching dresses. People enjoyed her dash. She was nicknamed "Her Serene Loveliness."

The youngest First Lady was Frances Cleveland, who was 21 when she married Grover Cleveland at the White House in 1886.

Grover Cleveland (1885-89, 1893-97)

Life doesn't stand still for the First Lady. Three women came to be First Lady as brides. Seven left the White House as widows. A dozen First Ladies had five children or more. Several had no children at all. Three First Ladies died during their husband's terms. First Ladies have had to cope with all the happy and sad events of life—with one big difference. The public is always watching.

The very first First Lady, Martha Washington, was shocked by her lack of privacy. She wrote, "I am more like a state prisoner than anything else." Since Washington's time, the news media have grown tremendously. First Ladies now have to cope with reporters and photographers, radio broadcasts and television interviews.

George Washington (1789-97)

Some First Ladies have actively enjoyed the public's attention; others have drawn back from

George and Martha Washington (at far right) at a social reception in the late 1700s

Dwight D. Eisenhower (1953-61)

it. During one year, Mamie Eisenhower shook about seven hundred hands a day. Women all over the country cut their hair in bangs just like Mamie's. They decorated their homes in her favorite color, pink. In contrast, First Lady Margaret Taylor spent most of her time upstairs in the private rooms. The American public did not even know what she looked like—and they still don't. No photos or paintings of her exist.

Zachary Taylor (1849-50)

Mamie Eisenhower

Gerald Ford (1974-77)

First Lady Betty Ford learned that the constant pressure of public attention could be put to good use. When she found out she had breast cancer, she told the public all about it. Her openness helped many women face their fear of cancer. Mrs. Ford said, "Lying in the hospital, thinking of all those women going for cancer checkups because of me, I'd come to recognize more clearly the power of the woman in the White House. Not my power, but the power of the position, a power which could be used to help."

Betty Ford

James Madison (1809-17)

Franklin D. Roosevelt (1933-45)

Two of the most successful First Ladies were Dolley Madison and Eleanor Roosevelt. Although they lived in the White House more than a century apart, these two women had much in common. Both of them loved meeting people, and people loved them in return. Eleanor Roosevelt once told a group of law students, "You will never get the greatest joy of living until you feel you are one with a great many people—a whole country perhaps."

The weekly White House reception (right) hosted by Dolley Madison (above) was so popular that it was nicknamed "Mrs. Madison's crush."

So many people came to the Madisons' weekly open house that it was called "Mrs. Madison's crush." Dolley Madison moved freely through the crowd, talking and joking with everyone. One senator complained that Mrs. Madison mixed high officials with lowly office workers—"greasy boots with silk stockings." But Dolley Madison treated each person with dignity.

Although she could talk on almost any subject, Dolley Madison did not talk politics. She was very tactful—she knew what not to say. During James Madison's term, France and England were at war with each other. On Madison's inauguration day, both the French minister and the English minister came for dinner. Everyone wondered which one would get the seat of honor beside the First Lady. Dolley Madison plunked down right between the two. They enjoyed a peaceful meal.

Franklin and Eleanor Roosevelt

Eleanor Roosevelt had the same gift of putting people at ease. Her husband, Franklin Delano Roosevelt, used a wheelchair because his legs were paralyzed. Eleanor Roosevelt decided to become his "extra eyes and ears." The Roosevelts were in the White House during World War II. Eleanor crossed both oceans to visit American troops. She was gone so much that President Roosevelt began to call her "Rover." On one trip, she talked to about four thousand American soldiers fighting in the South Pacific. An admiral went with her. He described a visit to an army

Mrs. Roosevelt with a group of American soldiers during World War II

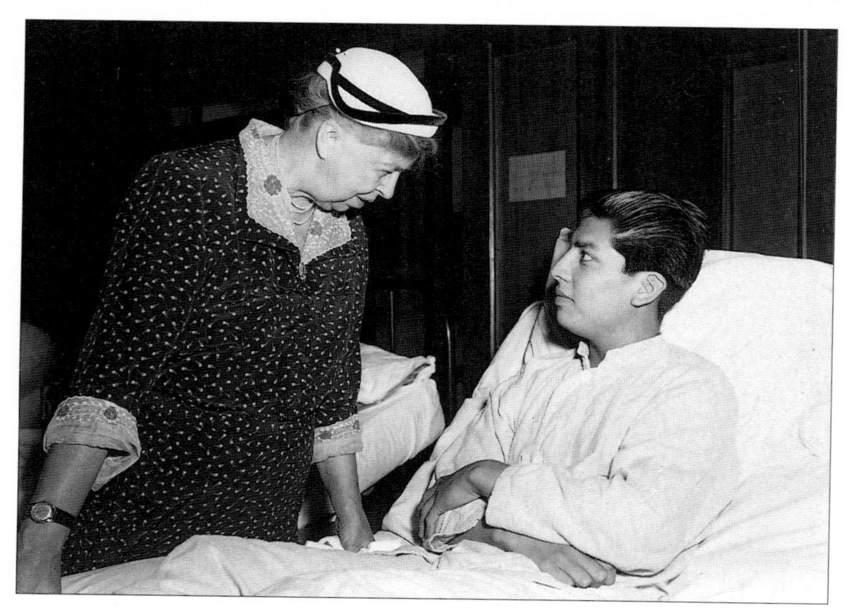

Mrs. Roosevelt visiting with a wounded U.S. soldier at the Tokyo Army Hospital

hospital: "She went into every ward, stopped at every bed, and spoke to every patient: What was his name? How did he feel? Was there anything he needed? Could she take a message home for him? . . . She alone had accomplished more good than any other person . . . who had passed through my area."

Both of these First Ladies carried out the role with energy, spirit, and warmth. They seemed to have just the right personalities for their times. Not every First Lady has been such a good match. Some have been crushed by illness or sorrow. Others have simply been out of step with their times. A few First Ladies have been hated; others have been simply ignored.

Franklin Pierce (1853-57)

Jane Pierce came to the White House in a mood of sadness that never lifted. Two months before Pierce's inauguration, the couple's only living son died in a railroad accident. Jane Pierce

Jane Pierce never got over the death of her son Benny, shown here with his mother in 1850.

never got over his death. She was not able to act as hostess. Once, halfway through her husband's term, she came down to greet people at a New Year's Day open house. Her effort was not a success. One guest wrote, "Her woe-begone face, with its sunken dark eyes, and skin like yellow ivory, banished all animation in others."

William McKinley (1897-1901)

First Lady Ida McKinley insisted on being part of everything even though she often had severe headaches and seizures. She always sat beside

William and Ida McKinley were extremely devoted to one another.

her husband at state dinners. If he saw her face twist in a seizure, he just covered her face with his handkerchief. When the seizure passed, she would pick up talking exactly where she had left off. Ida McKinley was demanding, irritable, and jealous. Her weakness was a constant strain for the president. When President McKinley was fatally shot by an assassin, he gasped, "My wife, be careful how you tell her!" When she found out, Ida McKinley surprised everyone. She was calm and strong all through the funeral. She lived another six years and never had another seizure.

Abraham Lincoln (1861-65)

Perhaps the most unpopular First Lady was Mary Todd Lincoln. Mary Lincoln was a very talented, bright woman. But she was also very worried about what people thought of her. She had a bad temper. She was easily insulted and her moods changed fast. One staff member wondered how she could change so quickly from being kind to being "so unreasonable, so irritable . . . so prone to see the dark, the wrong side of men and women and events."

Mary Todd Lincoln loved to buy expensive gowns.

During Mrs. Lincoln's time in the White House, the Civil War divided the country. Most of the

Mary Todd Lincoln and her family

First Lady's family fought on the Confederate side. Mary Lincoln herself was loyal to her husband and the Union. But this did not stop people from calling her a traitor. When she was upset, Mary Lincoln bought clothes—very expensive clothes. Her gorgeous gowns angered the American people, who were doing without things because of the war. President Lincoln didn't know how much his wife was spending. In four years, she ran up a frightening debt of twenty-seven thousand dollars.

Mary Lincoln was finally broken by the death of her eleven-year-old son, Will, in 1862. Her behavior became stranger and stranger. She believed she saw her son's ghost every night. She tried to talk with the dead. Even her husband had to admit that she might be insane.

When President Lincoln was assassinated, Americans grieved tremendously, but many had little sympathy for the First Lady. They felt she had caused her husband much suffering. Mary Lincoln did not have the inner strength or the toughness to be First Lady in such difficult times. She had made mistakes that made her a target for the nation's fear and anger. Moreover, the attention of the public made it even harder for her to deal with her deep personal sorrows.

In some ways, every First Lady has to rebuild the role to suit her own personality, her own tastes, her own style. However, until fairly

Lucy Hayes (far left), wife of Rutherford B. Hayes, (1877-81), was nicknamed "Lemonade Lucy" because she banned liquor at the White House. Caroline Harrison (left) helped raise funds for the Johns Hopkins University medical school on the condition that it admit women.

recently, First Ladies avoided even the appearance of power or independence. The list of First Ladies includes many bright, well-educated, and able women. Yet many of them were simply hostesses and housekeepers during their husband's presidencies. Caroline Harrison, for example, was a thoughtful and well-educated First Lady. Still, she is best remembered for painting a White House china pattern and bringing in the first White House Christmas tree.

Benjamin Harrison (1889-93)

First Ladies were traditionally reticent—they kept their opinions to themselves. They didn't campaign, make speeches, or meddle with politics. Throughout much of American history, most people believed that a woman's place was in the home, even if home was the White House. In

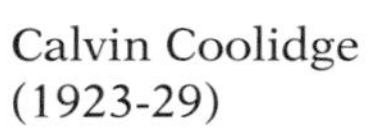
Calvin Coolidge (1923-29)

the 1920s, First Lady Grace Coolidge refused to make any speeches. When reporters put her on the spot, she jokingly used sign language. Politics were still off-limits for the First Lady. Why?

Some First Ladies probably shared the views of their times about a woman's place in society. Traditionally, the First Lady accepted that her role was to support her husband and do everything she could to further his political career. Winning the presidency can take years of work by husband, wife, and family. Many political wives have had to raise children, manage finances, and maintain family life in spite of frequent moves, campaign travel, and public attention.

Grace Coolidge

While many First Ladies carefully stayed out of

Grace Coolidge with her husband Calvin and their sons John and Calvin, Jr.

Abigail Adams was very involved in her husband's presidency.

John Adams (1797-1801)

politics, there were a few, beginning with Abigail Adams, who acted as working partners in their husbands' presidencies. Abigail Adams was a very able woman. She raised five children and ran the Adamses' family farm. But Abigail Adams did not limit herself to domestic life. She followed politics closely, formed strong opinions, and made no secret of them. She was both sharp-witted and sharp-tongued. She expected her husband to seek and value her opinions. She was unpleasantly surprised, however, when newspapers of the day attacked her as well as the president.

Sarah Polk and James Polk

The next presidential couple with a relationship like that of John and Abigail Adams was James and Sarah Polk. The Polks were one of the hardest-working couples to live in the White House. Unlike many First Ladies, Sarah Polk did not redecorate the White House. She remarked, "I will neither keep house, nor make butter. . . . I always take a deep interest in state and national affairs."

James Polk
(1845-49)

Sarah worked as her husband's personal assistant and closest advisor. A great reader, Sarah sifted through newspapers and reports. She picked out what she felt the president should read. She often went to hear debates in Congress, and enjoyed discussing politics. The Polks worked long hours and took no vacations. Overwork probably led to James Polk's death only three months after they left the White House. Sarah survived him by forty-two years.

William Howard Taft (1909-13)

Andrew Johnson (1865-69)

Helen Taft was another powerful First Lady, but only Washington insiders knew how powerful. She decided early on in her marriage that her husband was presidential material. She helped guide his career accordingly—moving with their three children from Ohio to Washington, D.C.; then back to Ohio; then to the Philippines where Taft was governor-general for four years; then back to Washington so Taft could serve as U.S. secretary of war; and, finally, to the White House.

Years before her husband became president, Elizabeth Johnson taught him reading and math.

Helen Herron Taft and William Howard Taft

The Tafts riding to the White House on Inauguration Day in 1909

Helen Taft was the first spouse to ride beside her husband in his carriage on Inauguration Day. Insiders knew that Mrs. Taft had tremendous influence over the president. She sat in on the White House meetings and joined political discussions. Taft always asked her opinion. Once, he jokingly wrote on a memo, “Memorandum for Mrs. Taft—the real president from the nominal president.” Yet publicly, Helen Taft downplayed her role. She said, “I do not believe in a woman meddling in politics or asserting herself along those lines, but I think any woman can discuss with her husband topics of national interest and, in many instances, she might give her opinion." Denying her real influence was simply good politics. A First Lady with too much power would make voters uneasy.

First Lady Edith Wilson found this out in 1919, when her husband, Woodrow Wilson, had two paralyzing strokes. Although Wilson's doctors said that the president's mind was as sharp as ever, he was very frail and physically helpless. The nation wondered if Wilson could handle the presidency. No law specified who should take over during a president's serious illness.

Edith Wilson stepped into the gap. For several

Edith Wilson and her husband, Woodrow Wilson

weeks, no one saw the president but his wife and his doctors. Edith Wilson had never before taken any interest in politics. Now she screened every question that came before the president. She alone decided what was important enough for him to see. She alone relayed his decisions back. If Edith Wilson thought it wasn't important, the president never found out about it. When people complained that this was bad for the country, Edith said, "I am not thinking of the country now, I am thinking of my husband."

Florence Harding, wife of President Warren Harding, was a driving force behind her husband's political career.

Many people were alarmed and frustrated by her control of the president and the country. After all, no one had voted for Edith Wilson. They had to take her word that the president was able to make decisions and that the wobbly signatures on bills and papers were really his. Some didn't believe her. Angry newspaper editorials suggested changing her title from First Lady to Acting First Man. Edith Wilson didn't see it that way. She wrote, "I never made a single decision regarding public affairs myself—the only decision that was mine was what was important and what not." Wilson gradually recovered, but the debate over Edith Wilson's stewardship still goes on.

Warren Harding (1921-23)

As attitudes towards women changed, people became more comfortable with the idea of an active and independent First Lady. Today, the American people still take an interest in what the

First Lady Eleanor Roosevelt inspecting a coal mine in Ohio (left) and visiting with schoolchildren in Puerto Rico (right)

First Lady wears, what her hobbies are, what kind of hostess she is, and how she decorates the White House. But over the years, the position of First Lady has developed into a platform for public accomplishment.

It was Eleanor Roosevelt who truly transformed the role of First Lady. She won acceptance for the idea of a First Lady who traveled alone, delivered her own speeches, and expressed her own ideas publicly. She even had her own daily syndicated newspaper column. Mrs. Roosevelt worked tirelessly to draw attention to the plight of worldwide victims of poverty, prejudice, and war. Her commitment set a new precedent; since her time, First Ladies

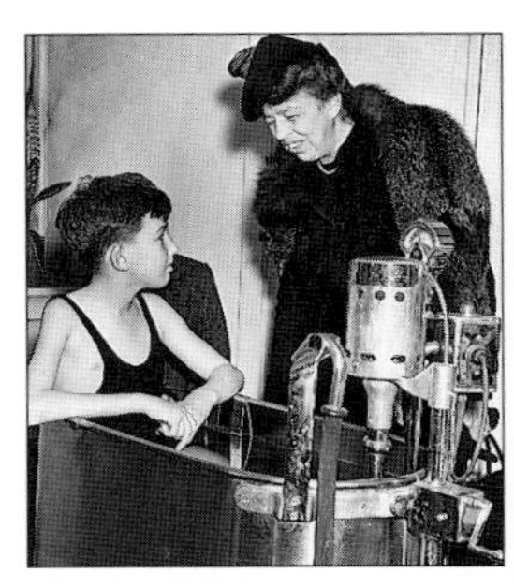

At a children's hospital, the First Lady chats with a boy recovering from polio.

Jacqueline Kennedy drew attention to the White House's importance as a historic landmark; Lady Bird Johnson planted trees to promote her "Beautification of America" project.

have increasingly used their position to draw public attention to social issues.

Jacqueline Kennedy, for example, helped stir national interest in the arts by bringing many cultural events to the White House, such as a concert by world-famous cellist Pablo Casals. Keenly aware of the White House's importance as a historic landmark, Mrs. Kennedy collected furnishings of past presidents and redecorated the mansion with these and other items of historical and artistic value. She also helped create the first guidebook for visitors to the White House.

Lady Bird Johnson focused attention on the "Beautification of America." She campaigned to

Lyndon B. Johnson (1963-69)

get rid of ugly billboards and junkyards along highways and supported plans to landscape public spaces. Her project led to new national laws. Lady Bird Johnson worked hard because she felt the pressure of time. As the First Ladies have become more politically active, they see their position in a new way—as an opportunity to get important things done. On leaving the White House, Lady Bird said, "I wish I could have worked harder and been more aggressive. It fitted my life to do all the things I did. I just wish I could have done more of them. There wasn't any more time or vigor."

Jimmy Carter (1977-81)

Rosalynn Carter made mental-health care her special project. She crossed the country gathering facts and making speeches, got experts in the field to help make plans, and presented her project to a congressional committee. The

First Lady Rosalynn Carter shakes hands with a Nicaraguan leader during a state visit to South America in 1979.

Nancy Reagan asked the nation's youth to "Just Say No" to drugs.

Carters made the First Lady a public official in a way she had never been before.

Like Sarah Polk, Rosalynn Carter worked closely with her husband. She read up on issues and acted as his private advisor. However, Rosalynn Carter's role shows how much the job changed; it was now official. Mrs. Carter had her own office, with a paid staff, in the East Wing of the White House. She also traveled alone to hold meetings with South American heads of state. She did not report on her trip simply to the president; she reported to the Senate.

Betty Ford, Nancy Reagan, and Barbara Bush each called attention to a specific issue of national concern. Betty Ford was an ardent supporter of the Equal Rights Amendment. Mrs.

Tackling illiteracy in America was Barbara Bush's special project.

Ronald Reagan (1981-89)

George Bush (1989-93)

Reagan made speeches and public-service announcements encouraging the nation's youth to "Just Say No!" to drugs. Barbara Bush tackled the issue of literacy—the ability to read. She learned that many people in America have trouble reading even a newspaper. Her travels and speeches drew attention to the problem. She encouraged new programs to teach reading. Her project improved the lives of many people.

Bill Clinton (1993-)

The most politically active First Lady to date is Hillary Rodham Clinton. Hillary Rodham and Bill Clinton met while both were law students at Yale University in the early 1970s. After the two married in 1975, Bill pursued politics, eventually becoming governor of Arkansas, while Hillary built a successful career as a lawyer. She became a senior partner in a major law firm, and was rated one of the top 100 attorneys in the nation. During his campaign for president in 1992, Bill Clinton promised that he and his wife would bring an "unprecedented partnership" to the White House. "Vote for one, get one free," they sometimes joked. When Bill Clinton won the election in 1992, Hillary Clinton left her job as a prominent, highly-paid attorney. She went to work for the president. She did not take the First Lady's traditional East Wing office, however. Instead, Hillary Clinton set up her office in the West Wing, with the president's most trusted and most powerful advisors.

Bill and Hillary Clinton at the MTV inaugural ball on January 20, 1993

Hillary Clinton speaking about health care

Although other First Ladies have chosen special projects, they have largely steered clear of the most troubling issues of their times. Hillary Clinton took on one of the central problems facing the nation: the need for health-care reform. All through his campaign, Bill Clinton promised to solve this problem. Once elected, he put the First Lady in charge of it. Hillary Clinton is the first First Lady to be an official policy maker. Like all First Ladies before her, however, she is still an unpaid volunteer.

Hillary Clinton is applauded just before President Clinton's first address to a joint session of Congress.

Three former First Ladies (clockwise from top left)—Bess Truman, Eleanor Roosevelt, and Edith Wilson—pose together in 1961.

Each First Lady has a chance to put her own personal stamp on the role. Perhaps that is why the First Lady is always so fascinating to the American people. The position changes with the historical times and the personality of each woman who holds it. Many First Ladies have worked very hard to reshape the role, to use its possibilities for the good of the country. Their energy, talent, and accomplishments have made the position of First Lady an ever more influential and engaging one.

INDEX

PHOTO CREDITS

Cover, George Bush Presidential Materials Project; 1, 2, © White House Historical Association (WHHA), photograph by the National Geographic Society; 3, UPI/Bettmann; 4 (top left, top right), © WHHA, photograph by the National Geographic Society; 4 (bottom), © WHHA, photograph by the National Geographic Society/U.S. Department of State; 5, Chicago Historical Society, neg. # ICHi-10543, photo by Pach Bros.; 6 (top left), AP/Wide World Photos; 6 (top right), © WHHA, photograph by the National Geographic Society/courtesy of Thomas J. Edwards and William K. Edwards; 6 (bottom), © WHHA, photograph by the National Geographic Society; 7 (top), UPI/Bettmann; 7 (bottom), © WHHA, photograph by the National Geographic Society; 8, The Daughters of the American Revolution Museum, Washington, D.C., Gift of Mrs. W.H. Park; 9 (top), © WHHA, photograph by the National Geographic Society; 9 (bottom), Wide World Photos; 10 (left), Courtesy of the Pennsylvania Academy of the Fine Arts, Philadelphia, Harrison Earl Fund; 10 (right), 11, 12, Stock Montage, Inc.; 13, © WHHA, photograph by the National Geographic Society/Pierce Brigade, Concord, NH; 14, 15 (bottom), Stock Montage, Inc.; 15 (top), The Bettmann Archive; 17, 18 (top), © WHHA, photograph by the National Geographic Society; 18 (bottom), AP/Wide World; 19, New York State Historical Association, Cooperstown; 20 (left), © WHHA, photograph by the National Geographic Society/Jame Knox Polk Memorial Association, Columbia, Tenn.; 20 (right), Stock Montage, Inc.; 21 (top, bottom left), © WHHA, photograph by the National Geographic Society; 21 (bottom right), William Howard Taft National Historic Site; 22, Library of Congress; 23, Stock Montage, Inc.; 24, © WHHA, photograph by the National Geographic Society; 25 (top left), The Bettmann Archive; 25 (top right, bottom), UPI/Bettmann; 26 (left), Wide World Photos; 26 (right), LBJ Library Collection; 27, UPI/Bettmann; 28 (top), Ronald Reagan Library; 28 (bottom), Bush Presidential Materials Project; 29, AP/Wide World; 30 (top), Reuters/Bettmann; 30 (bottom), Wide World Photos; 31, UPI/Bettmann

Picture Identifications:
Cover: Six First Ladies—Lady Bird Johnson, Pat Nixon, Nancy Reagan, Barbara Bush, Rosalynn Carter, and Betty Ford— pose together in 1991.
Page 1: A portrait of Julia Tyler, wife of President John Tyler
Page 2: A portrait of Martha Washington, America's first First Lady

Project Editor: Shari Joffe
Design: Karen Yops
Photo Research: Jan Izzo
Cornerstones of Freedom Logo: David Cunningham

ABOUT THE AUTHOR

Susan Maloney Clinton holds a Ph.D. in English and is a part-time teacher of English literature at Northwestern University. Her articles have appeared in such publications as *Consumer's Digest, Family Style Magazine,* and the Chicago *Reader*. In addition, she has contributed biographical and historical articles to *Encyclopaedia Britannica* and *Compton's Encyclopedia*. Ms. Clinton lives in Chicago with her husband, Pat, and their three children.